Other English colonies were settled in North America, such as Maryland, which was named after Charles I's wife Henrietta Maria, and New York, which was named after Charles II's brother the Duke of York. By 1732, Britain's **thirteen colonies** stretched along America's eastern coast from New Hampshire in the north, to Georgia in the south.

Native Americans

The English colonisation of North America was a catastrophe for its **indigenous** population. At first, English settlers depended upon the help of Native Americans to survive, and often traded European goods with them. But many English settlers saw Native American tribes as simple 'savages', and became increasingly brutal in their treatment of them.

But it was European diseases such as smallpox, influenza and diphtheria that had the most devastating impact. The population of Native American tribes living across North America plummeted, from an estimated 2 million in 1500, to just 325 000 in 1820.

Modern illustration of Native Americans trading with New England colonists during the 1600s

Caribbean

During this period, England's most profitable colonies were not in North America, but in the Caribbean. One of England's first Caribbean colonies was the island of **Barbados**, for which Charles I granted a Royal Charter in 1627. In 1643, the English plantation owners introduced the South Asian sugar cane plant to Barbados. Sugar cane thrived in the Caribbean's hot and humid environment, and was used to create refined sugar, molasses and rum.

Nicknamed 'white gold', sugar made Caribbean plantation owners some of the wealthiest people in England. England quickly added to its Caribbean colonies, and by 1660 had a string of islands including Antigua, Nevis, and Jamaica – which England seized from Spain in 1655. By 1775, Britain's sugar trade was worth five times more than the tobacco trade.

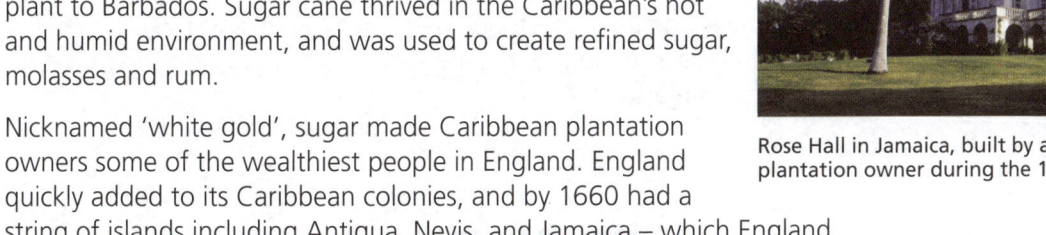

Rose Hall in Jamaica, built by a wealthy sugar plantation owner during the 1770s

Farming sugar cane, however, was very labour intensive. British workers, many of them convicts shipped to the Caribbean as punishment, were unable to withstand the Caribbean climate, and often died from diseases such as yellow fever or malaria. The solution to this shortage of labour was simple: African slaves.

Check your understanding

1. Which European countries established the first successful overseas empires?
2. When was North America first colonised by the English?
3. Who were the first settlers in New England?
4. What was the effect of European colonisation on the Native American population?
5. Why were England's Caribbean colonies so profitable?

Chapter 1: America

Unit 1: The British Empire
India

During the 16th century, European merchants began trading directly with what was perhaps the world's wealthiest region: India.

At this time, most of the Indian subcontinent was ruled by the Mughal Emperor. The **Mughals** were originally Muslim warlords from Central Asia, who conquered India during the 1550s. The Mughal Emperor granted each province of India to a prince, known as a *nawab*, to rule on his behalf.

European merchants competed for their share of the valuable trade in Indian sugar, saltpetre, indigo dye, and – most importantly – high-quality cotton and silk. However, European merchants first had to gain permission from the Mughal Emperor and his local *nawab*. First the Portuguese, then the Dutch, and finally the English and French were all given permission to trade, and built fortified trading posts known as **factories** along India's coastline.

The Red Fort, centre of Mughal rule in India

In 1600, Queen Elizabeth gave a royal charter to the **East India Company**. Over the course of the 17th century, the East India Company was given permission to trade in India at three major factories: Bombay (Mumbai) in India's northwest, Madras (Chennai) in the southeast, and Calcutta (Kolkata) in the northeastern province of **Bengal**. Unlike the settler colonies of the Americas, the East India Company's factories were built solely for trade. British merchants paid little attention to the interior of the vast country that lay beyond their coastal fortresses.

Diamond Pitt

Thomas Pitt travelled to India in 1674 to make his fortune. Despite working for the East India Company, he conducted his own private trade outside company business. In 1701, Pitt acquired a 410-carat diamond, then the largest in the world, and sold it in 1717 to the French royal family for five times its original price. Merchants who made their fortune in India were nicknamed 'nabobs', and this deal made 'Diamond Pitt' one of the richest nabobs in England.

Fact

The Mughal Emperor governed India from the Red Fort in Delhi, where he sat on a magnificent golden throne. The back of the throne represented an unfolding peacock tail, encrusted with rubies, diamonds and other precious stones.

British expansion

By the 1740s, the central power of the Mughal Emperor in India was breaking down. Afghan armies were invading India from the North, and across India, *nawabs* were breaking from Mughal authority and establishing their own independent kingdoms.

Collins

Key Stage 3
Modern Britain

The British Empire

CHAPTER 1:
America 2

CHAPTER 2:
India 4

CHAPTER 3:
Australia 6

CHAPTER 4:
Ruling the waves 8

CHAPTER 5:
Wealth and trade 10

Knowledge organiser 12

Quiz questions 14

Robert Peal

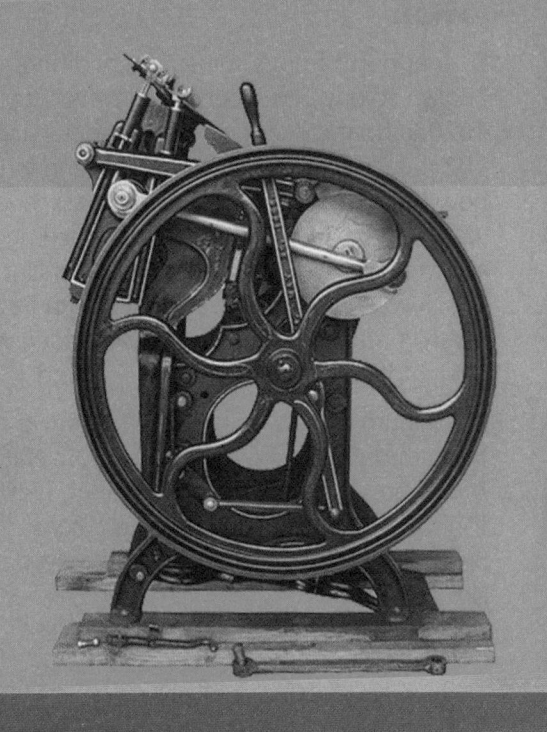

Knowing History

Unit 1: The British Empire
America

From 1600 to 1900, Britain built the largest empire the world has ever seen. At its peak, the British Empire governed a quarter of the world's landmass, and one fifth of its population.

The journeys made by European explorers at the end of the 15th century gave birth to a new age of European empire. At first, Spain led the way by establishing new colonies in the Americas, such as Mexico and Peru. Portugal developed the most extensive trading routes, spreading from Brazil to Indonesia. And the Netherlands pioneered an advanced banking system for investing in overseas trade.

In comparison with its European neighbours, England lagged well behind.

Settlement

At the beginning of the 17th century, however, the English began to establish their own colonies in the Americas. England's first successful colony was **Virginia** in North America. Like many early colonies, Virginia was settled by a private company. The Virginia Company was granted a Royal Charter by King James I in 1606 to explore and cultivate North American territories. English settlers built large farms in Virginia, called plantations, but struggled to find the right crop for the soil and climate – some even tried to plant olive groves!

A breakthrough came in 1617 when the English settlers discovered that the tobacco plant grew well in Virginia. Soon, enormous tobacco plantations were spreading across the colony, and by 1700 almost 6 million kilograms of Virginian tobacco was being exported to Britain each year.

Further north from Virginia, a very different English colony developed. On 9 November 1620, a boat called the *Mayflower* carrying 102 passengers landed at Cape Cod in what is now Massachusetts. Many of the passengers were Puritans, who wanted to escape England and create a community of perfect godliness in the New World. Known as the **Pilgrim Fathers**, these Puritan settlers named their colder, wetter stretch of North America 'New England'.

The Pilgrim Fathers established a lucrative trade through buying animal furs from Native American tribes, and fishing the abundant fishing stocks off America's eastern coast. By 1640, 20000 more settlers had arrived in New England.

Fact

England's first American colony was founded in 1587 with 116 people. The colony was named 'Roanoke', and its governor John White returned to England after one month to collect more supplies. White was unable to return to Roanoke until 1590. When he finally reached the colony, its settlers had disappeared. To this day, the mystery of the 'lost colony' of Roanoke has never been solved.

Modern illustration of the Pilgrim Fathers leaving Plymouth for America

In response to this confusion, the East India Company began to fortify its coastal factories. The Company built its own army, recruiting troops from India's warrior castes and British officers to lead them. During the 1750s, the Company became involved in the power struggles of competing Indian nawabs, often fighting battles against rival *nawabs* backed by the French East India Company.

In 1756, Bengal gained a new *nawab*, Siraj ud-Daulah, who resented the growing size of Calcutta, Britain's trading port in Bengal. In June 1756, Siraj seized Calcutta from the British. News of the loss of Calcutta spread south to Madras, where an ambitious young army officer in the East India Company Army named Robert Clive decided to take action.

Clive marched his army 1000 miles north from Madras to relieve Calcutta. A canny politician as well as a talented soldier, Clive persuaded Siraj's commander, Mir Jafar, to betray his own *nawab*. At the **Battle of Plassey** on 23 June, 1757, Clive's combination of Indian soldiers and European weapons proved brutally effective. With just 3000 troops, he defeated Siraj's army of 50 000 men. Clive then installed Mir Jafar as a 'puppet' *nawab* of Bengal.

Contemporary painting of Robert Clive meeting with Mir Jafar after the Battle of Plassey

At the **Treaty of Allahabad** in 1765, the Mughal Emperor placed the province of Bengal under the direct rule of the East India Company, with Robert Clive as Governor. This turning point marks the beginning of the British Empire in India. It gave the East India Company the right to tax 20 million people, making around £3 million a year. For the Company, territory and taxation would prove to be even more profitable than trade.

Following the Treaty of Allahabad, the East India Company Army grew to over 100 000 men, and continued to expand the boundaries of its power across India. This process was driven by opportunistic army officers, such as Clive, who acted with a great deal of independence from the British government and company directors back in London – many of whom were opposed to the growing political power of the East India Company.

By 1815, the East India Company ruled much of northeast India, spreading from Bengal towards Delhi; the entire eastern coast from Calcutta in the north to the Carnatic in the south; and a growing portion of southwest India. Around 40 million Indians were living directly under British rule, including – from 1803 onwards – the Mughal Emperor himself. In the place of the crumbling Mughal Empire, the Governor General of the East India Company was now the *de facto* ruler of much of India.

Statue of Robert Clive in Whitehall, London

Check your understanding

1. Who ruled India during the 16th and 17th centuries?
2. Where did the East India Company conduct its trade during the 17th century?
3. What was happening to the Mughal Empire by the 1740s?
4. Why was the Treaty of Allahabad a turning point in the history of the British in India?
5. How far had British rule in India spread by 1815?

Unit 1: The British Empire
Australia

On 26 August, 1768, the British government sent a naval captain called James Cook to explore the South Pacific Ocean on board a ship named the *Endeavour*.

Part of Cook's mission was to claim for Britain a mysterious continent in the South Pacific Ocean which had been encountered by European sailors, but so far lay unexplored. It was known as *Terra Australis*, Latin for 'Southern land'.

Captain Cook grew up the son of a poor farm labourer in Yorkshire, and left home aged seventeen to work at sea. Cook joined the Royal Navy in 1755, and despite his poor background was quickly promoted through the ranks. Intelligent and hard-working, Cook taught himself Greek, geometry and astronomy – all subjects needed to be able to navigate at sea. By 1768, Cook had gained a reputation as the most able navigator in the Royal Navy.

From 1769 to 1770, Cook sailed around the two islands of New Zealand, and mapped its coastline. The *Endeavour* then continued west to the southeastern tip of Australia, where in April 1770 Cook anchored in a large bay. One member of his crew – an enthusiastic botanist called Joseph Banks – went onshore in search of new plant species. Banks found so many new specimens that Cook named their landing site 'Botany Bay'. The *Endeavour* then continued along the eastern shore of Australia, as Cook drew a detailed map of its coastline.

On 11 June, the *Endeavour* struck the Great Barrier Reef, and began to sink. The crew only managed to keep the ship afloat by plugging the hole with an old sail, and landing again on the Australian coast to carry out urgent repairs. On 13 September 1770, Cook claimed Australia for King George III, and the patched-up *Endeavour* returned to Britain. After three years at sea, Cook was welcomed home a national hero.

Portrait of Captain James Cook

Settlement

On returning to Britain, Joseph Banks suggested to Parliament that they could solve the problem of Britain's overcrowded prisons by using Australia as a **penal colony**. Parliament agreed.

On 13 May 1788, the First Fleet of 11 convict ships reached Australia. Along with their prison guards, the ships carried 543 male convicts, and 189 female.

Contemporary illustration of the landing of convicts at Botany Bay

The convicts were settled in a cove north of Botany Bay, which was named Sydney after the Government Minister who had sanctioned the colony. Over the next 80 years, around 161 000 convicts were deported from Britain to work as prisoners in Australia.

> ### Death of Captain Cook
>
> In 1776, Cook embarked on his third Pacific voyage, and he landed with his crew on the island of Hawaii in January 1779. They were the first Europeans to visit Hawaii, and the islanders welcomed Cook as a god, throwing a lavish festival in his honour. But as the visitors outstayed their welcome, relations soured. During an argument over a stolen boat, Captain Cook was caught by the islanders and clubbed to death.

Convicts were usually sentenced to seven years of forced labour, often for crimes as minor as stealing chickens from a farm. However, those convicts who survived their sentence were able to start a new life in Australia. Former convicts were granted free land to farm, and many played an important role in the early life of the country.

Over the course of the 19th century, Australia was transformed from a penal colony into a prosperous outpost of the British Empire. Much of this wealth was due to the introduction of merino sheep from Spain, whose fine wool was highly sought after in Europe. What sugar was to Barbados, wool was to Australia. By 1821 there were 38 000 people, and 290 000 sheep on the island.

As the British settlers in Australia prospered, however, the indigenous population suffered terribly. Known as **Aborigines**, they were a nomadic hunter-gatherer people, who had inhabited Australia for at least 50 000 years. But just like the Native Americans, Aborigines were devastated by conflict with the Europeans, and diseases such as smallpox.

As British settlers claimed Aboriginal hunting lands, more Aborigines starved or died in long running battles with the colonists. The worst abuses occurred on the island of Tasmania, where British settlers hunted and systematically killed the native population until – in 1876 – there was not a single Aborigine left on the island.

Many in Britain were appalled by the fate of the Aborigines, and Parliament appointed an Aboriginal Protector to Australia in 1838. Despite this, it has been estimated that between 1788 and 1900, Australia's Aboriginal population decreased by 90 per cent.

> ### Fact
>
> Mary Reibey was convicted of horse stealing in Lancashire at the age of 13 in 1790, and transported as a convict to Australia. Having served her sentence, Reibey became a successful hotel-owner, moneylender, and businesswoman. By 1820, she had accumulated a fortune of £20 000.

Australian Aborigines using traditional methods to catch fish

Check your understanding
1. How did James Cook rise to become a Captain in the Royal Navy?
2. What did Captain Cook achieve on his first voyage to the Pacific Ocean?
3. Who were the first British settlers in Australia?
4. What became the source of Australia's early wealth as a colony?
5. How did the British settlers treat the indigenous population in Australia?

Unit 1: The British Empire
Ruling the waves

British merchants needed the Royal Navy to protect them from foreign attacks, so that they could trade safely with Britain's overseas colonies.

As an island nation, Britain had long been proud of its navy. However, by the 1740s the Royal Navy was in a dire condition, and suffered a string of embarrassing defeats at the hands of the French and Spanish.

The man charged with reforming the Royal Navy was a battle-hardened **Admiral** called George Anson. Made **First Lord of the Admiralty** in 1751, Lord Anson introduced sweeping reforms. He took control of the marines from the army, giving the Royal Navy a crack force of soldiers who could fight both on land and at sea. He also introduced a uniform for naval officers, consisting of a blue coat and white breeches. And he greatly increased naval discipline. This new level of discipline was revealed in 1756, when Admiral Byng lost Britain's important Mediterranean colony of Minorca. Back in England, the 52-year-old Admiral was shot by firing squad.

George Anson, First Lord of the Admiralty who reformed the Royal Navy

Most importantly, Anson persuaded the government to invest in new, state of the art ships. Britain's enormous dockyards in Portsmouth, Plymouth, Deptford and Chatham employed thousands of men, building large 74-gun battleships for naval wars, and smaller 36-gun frigates for scouting and protecting merchant ships. The 104-gun HMS *Victory*, which was launched in 1765, took 6000 trees to build.

Seven Years' War

The **Seven Years' War** began in 1756, and was the world's first truly global conflict. The war was mainly fought between Britain and France, but fighting spread across the world to their colonies. Battles were fought in North America, the Caribbean, Africa and India – where Robert Clive won his victory at Plassey in 1757 (see pages 4–5).

HMS *Victory*, today preserved as a museum in Portsmouth

In 1759, Britain launched an attack on **Quebec**, the capital of the French possessions in North America (part of present-day Canada). With the help of the Royal Navy, 4600 troops under the leadership of General Wolfe sailed up the St Lawrence River towards Quebec at night. On 13 September, they took the city in a surprise attack. General Wolfe was killed, but his victory gave Britain almost complete control of North America.

Fact

Sailors who did not follow orders risked being flogged by the cat o' nine tails, a whip made of nine knotted leather cords, designed to cut the skin.

Later that year on 20 November, the Royal Navy defeated the French Navy off the coast of France at the Battle of **Quiberon Bay**. The French were planning to invade Britain, but the Royal Navy intercepted a fleet of 27 ships. Six French ships were destroyed, and one was captured.

The Royal Navy went on to capture Havana and Manila (in the Philippines) from the Spanish, and a number of French islands in the Caribbean. When the Treaty of Paris was signed with the French in 1763, Britain had expanded its power in India, taken French territories in North America and the Caribbean, and retained its power in the Mediterranean by keeping **Gibraltar** and Minorca.

The end of the Seven Years' War marked the beginning of Britain's global dominance, which would last 150 years. At the root of this dominance lay the Royal Navy. By 1800, the British had 285 major battleships in service around the world, more than the French, Spanish, Dutch and Danish fleets combined.

Life as a British seaman

The Royal Navy grew from around 12 000 men during the early 18th century, to 85 000 men in 1763, and 150 000 by 1815.

Naval ships could go for months without touching dry land, so it was impossible to eat fresh food. Seamen lived off a diet of meat preserved in salt, and dry biscuits which were often riddled with worms and insects. The lack of vitamin C in a sailor's diet meant many suffered from **scurvy**, a disease which caused their gums to rot, teeth to fall out, and bodies to become covered in ulcers. Scurvy killed far more seamen than active combat during the 18th century. Recruiting enough men to join the navy could be difficult, so **press gangs** visited towns and cities along the British coast and forced sailors to join.

However, service in the Royal Navy did hold some opportunities. When an enemy merchant ship was captured, the prize money would be shared out among the crew, and naval seamen liked to flaunt their wealth with colourful clothing and gold earrings. Royal Navy seamen were nicknamed 'Jack Tars'. Some would cover their arms in naval tattoos, a practice learned from the tribespeople Captain Cook encountered in Tahiti. And their drink of choice was rum. Made from Caribbean sugar, British sailors were entitled to a ration of half a pint of rum a day.

Contemporary illustration of a British soldier being flogged with a cat o' nine tails.

Check your understanding

1. Why was the Royal Navy in need of reform after the 1740s?
2. What reforms did Lord Anson make to the Royal Navy from 1751?
3. In what parts of the world was the Seven Years' War fought?
4. Why did the end of the Seven Years' War mark the start of Britain's role as a global power?
5. Why did so many seamen in the Royal Navy die of scurvy?

Unit 1: The British Empire
Wealth and trade

As trade between Britain and its colonies developed and the volume of foreign **imports** increased, their prices dropped dramatically.

In 1620 smoking was a luxury confined to the upper classes, as a pound of tobacco cost 36 pennies. By the 1660s, a pound of tobacco cost just one penny. A doctor, Thomas Tryon, complained in 1691: "Now every plow-man has his pipe to himself."

Sugar became Britain's biggest import during the 18th century, growing from 20 million kg in 1650 to 400 million kg in 1820. At the end of the 18th century, an English writer estimated that workers in southern England were spending 11 per cent of their wages on sugar, treacle and tea.

The amount of tea imported from China by the East India Company increased from 1 million kg in 1720 to 14.5 million kg in 1790. Though tea is drunk on its own in China, the British took to combining it with milk and sugar, creating a national drink that persists to this day. Sugar was combined with spices from the Far East such as ginger, nutmeg and cinnamon to create dishes we now see as typically British: cakes, spiced buns and chutneys.

Colonial trade also changed how people dressed. At the beginning of the 18th century, a couple from a modest background would have dressed exclusively in linen and woollen cloth produced in Britain, often of dull colours. By the end of the 18th century, a woman could wear fine cotton textiles or Chinese silk, while her husband could wear a fashionable tricorn hat made from Canadian beaver fur. These clothes would have been noticeably more colourful, thanks to imported dyes such as indigo.

Goods which had once been seen as luxuries had become necessities. To house these goods, the number of shops in Britain exploded from 50 000 in 1688 to 162 000 in 1759. Some historians claim that Britain became a **consumer society** for the first time during the 18th century.

> **Fact**
>
> The wealthy took their tea in finely made white porcelain imported from China, which was prized for its thinness. This porcelain became known, unsurprisingly, as 'china'.

Mr and Mrs Andrews, painted by Thomas Gainsborough around 1750, wearing clothing made fashionable by Empire

Mercantilism

During this period, European countries did not trade freely with one another. They protected their own trade, and discouraged trade with their European rivals. This was a policy known as **mercantilism**.

A series of laws passed at the end of the 17th century called the Navigation Acts established how trade in the British Empire would function. All trade to

10   Unit 1: The British Empire

and from British colonies had to be carried in British ships. Taxes known as **customs duties** were placed on imports from other European countries, to encourage trade with the Empire.

Mercantilism made Britain the centre of global trade. Goods from British colonies in America, Asia and the Pacific all had to pass through British ports before continuing their journey to other parts of Europe, allowing British merchants to make a tidy profit. By 1770, 85 per cent of tobacco that arrived in Britain was re-exported to other parts of the world, as was 94 per cent of coffee.

Ports such as London, Bristol, Liverpool and Glasgow were Britain's fastest growing cities during this period. By the mid-18th century, 6000 merchant ships were coming in and out of these ports – twice the number of merchant ships in France.

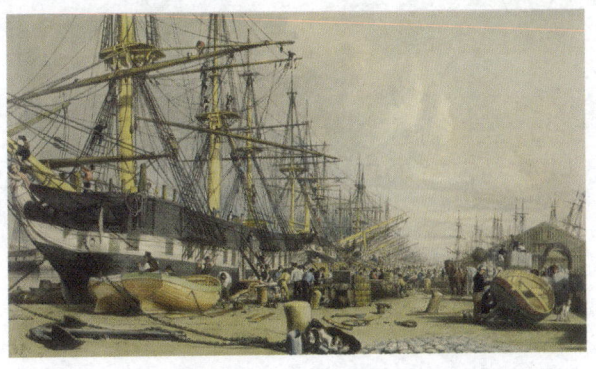

Painting of goods being unloaded at the West India Docks in London, 1840

British identity

The nation of Britain was only formed through the 1707 Act of Union, which united England and Scotland. During the years that followed, a British national identity began to form around Britain's role as a global power. The Scottish and Irish played a major role in building Britain's Empire. It has been estimated that three quarters of all British settlers in overseas colonies after 1700 came from either Scotland or Ireland, and half of those who served in the East India Company were Scottish.

The female figure of **Britannia**, with her Union Jack shield, came to symbolise the growing **patriotism** in Britain. In 1744, the first version of Britain's national anthem, 'God Save the King', was published. Politicians who appealed to the empire and patriotism could ensure great support, such as William Pitt who became Prime Minister during the Seven Years' War. Pitt knew the value of empire: his own family fortune came from his grandfather, the famous nabob 'Diamond Pitt', trading in India (see page 4).

Image of Britannia, on the reverse of the old 50p coin

In 1740, a song which was to become linked with the British Empire for generations was performed for the first time. Its chorus went:

> "Rule Britannia! Rule the waves:
> Britons never will be slaves."

These lyrics pointed to the dark heart of the British Empire. As you will learn in the next chapter, Britain's buoyant trade in consumer goods was built on African slavery.

Check your understanding

1. What consumer goods became widely available in Britain during the 18th century?
2. How did colonial trade change the way that people dressed?
3. How did the policy of mercantilism encourage trade with Britain's colonies?
4. What effect did colonial trade have on cities in Britain's cities?
5. How did a new British national identity emerge during the 18th century?

Chapter 5: Wealth and trade

Unit 1: The British Empire
Knowledge organiser

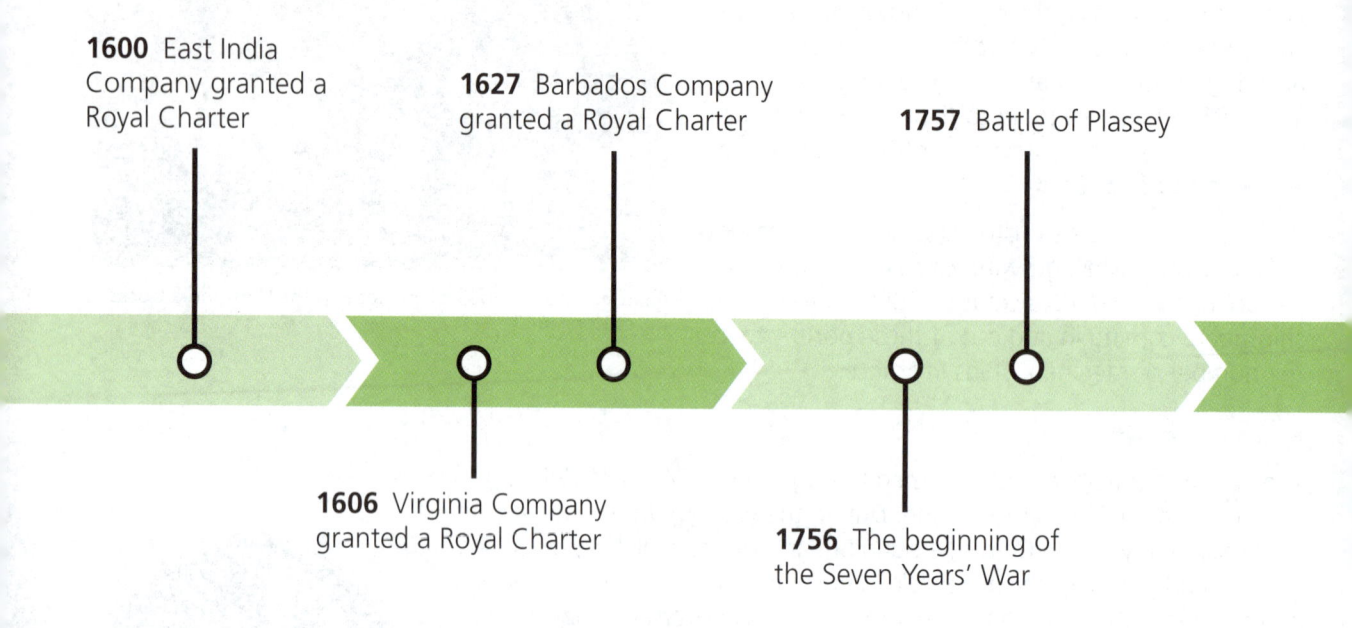

1600 East India Company granted a Royal Charter

1606 Virginia Company granted a Royal Charter

1627 Barbados Company granted a Royal Charter

1756 The beginning of the Seven Years' War

1757 Battle of Plassey

Key vocabulary

Aborigine Nomadic hunter-gatherer population native to Australia and nearby islands

Admiral Highest ranking naval officer, usually in command of a fleet

Barbados Caribbean island, and one of England's first major sugar-producing colonies

Battle of Plassey Key victory for Clive and the East India Company against the *nawab* of Bengal

Bengal Wealthy province in northeast India, where the British built their factory called Calcutta

Britannia A female figure, used to symbolise Britain and popular during the British Empire

Consumer society A society where people can afford to buy non-essential 'consumer' goods

Customs duties Taxes placed by a government on goods imported from foreign countries

East India Company Private company formed in 1600 with rights to trade between India and England

Endeavour The ship that Captain Cook sailed on his first voyage to Australia

Exports Goods or services sold to other countries

Factories (colonial) Coastal trading posts where merchants can do business in foreign lands

First Lord of the Admiralty Head of the Royal Navy

Gibraltar British colony at the southern tip of Spain, gained in 1713

Imports Goods or services brought in from other countries

Indigenous Originating in a particular place

Mayflower Ship that carried the first settlers to New England in 1620

Mercantilism The economic practice of discouraging trade with rival nations

Mughals Dynasty originally from Central Asia that ruled much of India from the 16th to 19th century

Nawab Prince granted a province of India to rule on behalf of the Mughal Emperor

Patriotism Showing strong support for your own country

Penal colony A remote settlement used to exile convicted criminals from the general population

1759 (September) Britain wins the Battle of Quebec

1765 Treaty of Allahabad

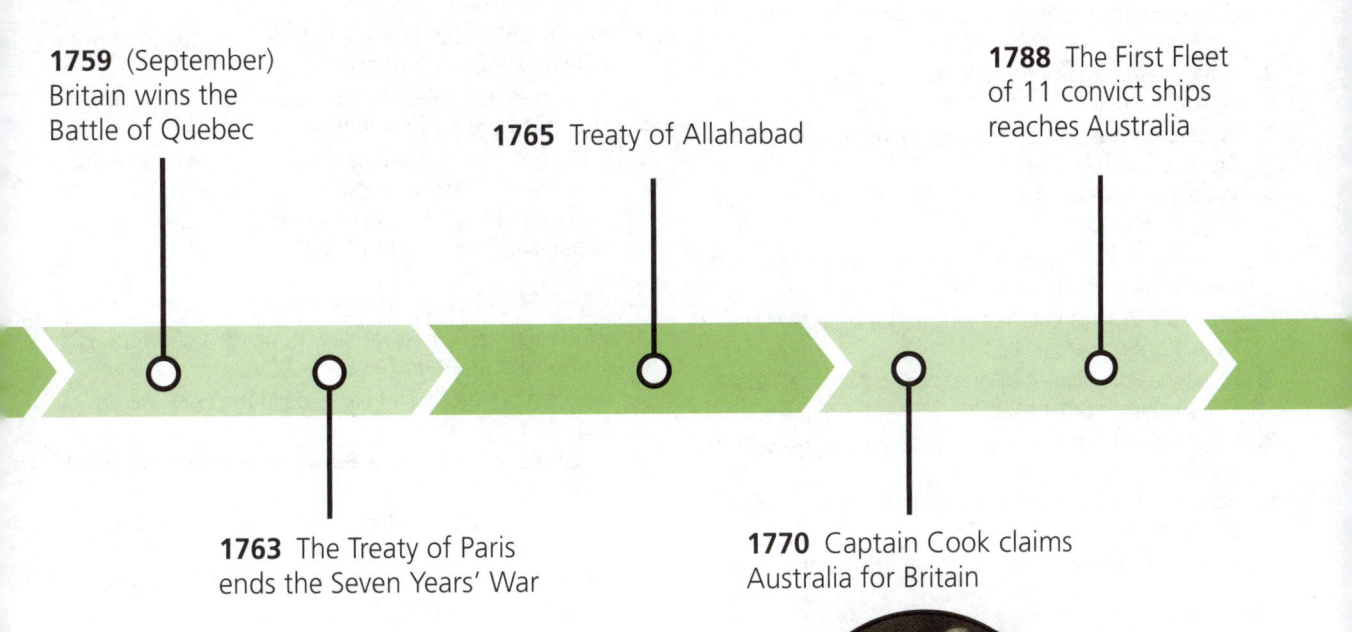

1788 The First Fleet of 11 convict ships reaches Australia

1763 The Treaty of Paris ends the Seven Years' War

1770 Captain Cook claims Australia for Britain

Key vocabulary

Pilgrim Fathers The first settlers in New England, known for their religious Puritanism

Press gangs Groups who would travel Britain forcing men to enlist in the Army or Navy

Quebec Capital of French possessions in America, now a city in present day Canada

Quiberon Bay Battle in which the British defeated the French navy, preventing invasion

Scurvy Disease caused by a lack of vitamin C, which killed many sailors in the Royal Navy

Seven Years' War Global conflict, which saw Britain emerge as a dominant world power

Thirteen colonies The original British settlements along the east coast of North America

Treaty of Allahabad Treaty granting government of Bengal province to the East India Company

Virginia The first English colony in North America, named after Elizabeth I

Key people

General Wolfe British army officer who led the capture of Quebec in 1759

George Anson First Lord of the Admiralty who introduced sweeping reforms to the Royal Navy

James Cook British explorer and navigator who mapped Australia's eastern coastline

Joseph Banks Botanist on board the *Endeavour* who studied Australia's plants and wildlife

Robert Clive Officer in the East India Company who became Governor of Bengal Province

Thomas Pitt British merchant in India, made his fortune selling the world's largest diamond

William Pitt British politician, made Prime Minister during the Seven Years' War

Knowledge organiser

Quiz questions

Chapter 1: America
1. Which European country first established colonies, such as Mexico, in the Americas?
2. What was England's first successful colony in North America?
3. What crop was successfully grown in this colony from 1617 onwards?
4. What ship transported the first English settlers to New England in 1620?
5. What were the first settlers in New England, known for their religious Puritanism, called?
6. What are Britain's colonies in America collectively called from 1732 onwards?
7. What was the biggest killer of Native American tribes living in North America?
8. Which island was England's first major sugar-producing colony?
9. How much more was the sugar trade worth compared to the tobacco trade by 1775?
10. What nickname was given to sugar in the British colonies?

Chapter 2: India
1. Which imperial dynasty ruled in India from the 16th to the 19th century?
2. What was a prince who ruled an Indian province on behalf of the Emperor called?
3. What English company formed in 1600 was granted exclusive rights to trade with India?
4. What was a trading post where merchants did business in foreign lands called?
5. Which British merchant in India made his fortune selling the world's largest diamond?
6. In which northeastern province of India did the British build their trading post, Calcutta?
7. Which British officer defeated Siraj ud-Daulah at the Battle of Plassey?
8. In what year was the Battle of Plassey?
9. What treaty granted Britain an Indian Province to rule for the first time?
10. How many Indians were living under British rule by 1815?

Chapter 3: Australia
1. Which British explorer and navigator mapped Australia's eastern coastline?
2. What was the name of his ship?
3. Which botanist studied Australia's plants and wildlife during this journey?
4. In what year was Australia claimed as a British colony?
5. What sort of colony did Australia become from 1788 onwards?
6. What term was used to describe the people forced to live in Australia?
7. How many of these people in total were deported from Britain to work in Australia?
8. What was Australia's most successful industry by the start of the nineteenth century?
9. What nomadic hunter-gatherer people were native to Australia and nearby islands?
10. What was the percentage decrease in Australia's native population from 1788 to 1900?

Chapter 4: Ruling the waves
1. Who reformed the Royal Navy from 1751 onwards as First Lord of the Admiralty?
2. How many trees did it take to build the HMS *Victory*, launched in 1765?
3. What global conflict saw Britain emerge as a dominant global power?
4. In what year was the Treaty of Paris signed, ending this conflict?
5. What North American city did General Wolfe capture from the French in 1759?
6. What colony at the southern tip of Spain was Britain allowed to keep after this treaty?
7. How many major battleships were in service for the Royal Navy by 1800?
8. How many men did the Royal Navy contain by 1815?
9. What groups travelled around Britain forcing men to enlist in the army or navy?
10. What disease caused by a lack of vitamin C killed many sailors in the Royal Navy?

Chapter 5: Wealth and trade
1. What was Britain's biggest import during the eighteenth century?
2. In 1790, Britain imported 14.5 million kg of what product from China?
3. What new materials could many more people wear due to colonial trade?
4. What popular item of Georgian clothing was made from Canadian beaver fur?
5. What term is used for a society where people can afford to buy non-essential goods?
6. What economic practice discourages trade with rival nations?
7. What taxes did the British government place on goods imported from foreign countries?
8. In 1770, what proportion of coffee that arrived in Britain was re-exported?
9. Which nation provided half the people who served in the East India Company?
10. Which female figure was used to symbolise the British Empire?

HarperCollins Publishers
200 — Since 1817

William Collins' dream of knowledge for all began with the publication of his first book in 1819. A self-educated mill worker, he not only enriched millions of lives, but also founded a flourishing publishing house. Today, staying true to this spirit, Collins books are packed with inspiration, innovation and practical expertise. They place you at the centre of a world of possibility and give you exactly what you need to explore it.

Collins. Freedom to teach

Published by Collins
An imprint of HarperCollins*Publishers*
The News Building
1 London Bridge Street
London SE1 9GF

Text © Robert Peal 2017
Design © HarperCollins*Publishers* 2017

10 9 8 7 6 5 4 3 2 1

ISBN 978-0-00-819538-0

Robert Peal asserts his moral right to be identified as the author of this work.

All rights reserved. No part of this book may be reproduced, stored in a retrieval system, or transmitted in any form or by any means, electronic, mechanical, photocopying, recording or otherwise, without the prior permission in writing of the Publisher. This book is sold subject to the conditions that it shall not, by way of trade or otherwise, be lent, re-sold, hired out or otherwise circulated without the Publisher's prior consent in any form of binding or cover other than that in which it is published and without a similar condition including this condition being imposed on the subsequent purchaser.

HarperCollins does not warrant that any website mentioned in this title will be provided uninterrupted, that any website will be error free, that defects will be corrected, or that the website or the server that makes it available are free of viruses or bugs. For full terms and conditions please refer to the site terms provided on the website.

A catalogue record for this book is available from the British Library

Publisher: Katie Sergeant
Editor: Hannah Dove
Author: Robert Peal
Fact-checker: Barbara Hibbert
Copy-editor: Sally Clifford
Image researcher: Alison Prior
Proof-reader: Ros and Chris Davies
Cover designer: Angela English
Cover image: typografie/Alamy
Production controller: Rachel Weaver
Typesetter: QBS
Printed and bound by Martins, UK

Acknowledgments

Every effort has been made to trace copyright holders and to obtain their permission for the use of copyright material. The publishers will gladly receive any information enabling them to rectify any error or omission at the first opportunity.

The publishers would like to thank the following for permission to reproduce copyright material:

(t = top, b = bottom, c = centre, l = left, r = right)

Cover & p1 typografie/Alamy; p2 Mary Evans Picture Library/Alamy; p3t North Wind Picture Archives/Alamy; p3b Danita Delimont/Alamy; p4t aravind chandramohanan/Alamy; p4b World History Archive/Alamy; p5b Pjr Tra\vel/Alamy; p5t Granger Historical Picture Archive; p6t G L Archive/Alamy; p6b Pictorial Press Ltd/Alamy; p7 Travel Pictures/Alamy; p8t INTERFOTO/Alamy; p8b Liquid Light/Alamy; p9 Florilegius/alamy; p10t Geffrye Museum/Alamy; p10b The Archives/Alamy; p11t Heritage Image Partnership Ltd/Alamy; p11b Sam Toren/Alamy; p13 G L Archive/Alamy

MIX — Paper from responsible sources
FSC® C007454

FSC™ is a non-profit international organisation established to promote the responsible management of the world's forests. Products carrying the FSC label are independently certified to assure consumers that they come from forests that are managed to meet the social, economic and ecological needs of present and future generations, and other controlled sources.

Find out more about HarperCollins and the environment at
www.harpercollins.co.uk/green

Collins

Key Stage 3
Modern Britain
The British Empire

The Knowing History unit booklets help you to:

- Think critically about the past by focusing on the knowledge you need and then checking your understanding.
- Learn history through extraordinary people, amazing facts, and a distinctly engaging narrative.
- Remember key dates, vocabulary and significant people with the 'Knowledge organiser'.
- Test your knowledge with 'Quiz questions' for each chapter.

Knowing History Modern Britain booklets

The British Empire	978-0-00-819538-0
The Americas	978-0-00-819539-7
The French Revolution	978-0-00-819540-3
The Industrial Revolution	978-0-00-819541-0
The Age of Reform	978-0-00-819542-7
The Victorian Empire	978-0-00-819543-4

The Modern Britain booklets are also available in:
Modern Britain 1760–1900 Student Book 3

Medieval Britain
410–1509
Student Book 1
978-0-00-819523-6

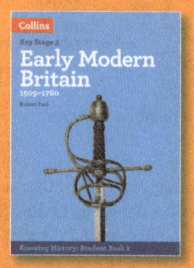

Early Modern Britain
1509–1760
Student Book 2
978-0-00-819524-3

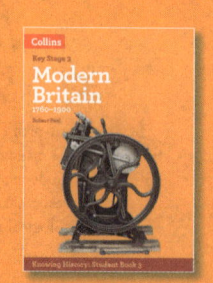

Modern Britain
1760–1900
Student Book 3
978-0-00-819525-0

Free Teacher Guides available on www.collins.co.uk

Collins
FREEDOM TO TEACH
Find us at www.collins.co.uk
and follow our blog – articles and information by teachers for teachers.
@FreedomToTeach

ISBN 978-0-00-819538-0

9 780008 195380